MW00958489

BLOOMSBURY CHILDREN'S BOOKS
Bloomsbury Publishing Plc
50 Bedford Square, London, WC1B 3DP, UK

BLOOMSBURY, BLOOMSBURY CHILDREN'S BOOKS and the Diana logo are
trademarks of Bloomsbury Publishing Plc

First published in Great Britain 2019 by Bloomsbury Publishing Plc

A catalogue record for this book is available from the British Library

ISBN: 978-1-4088-9638-9

2 4 6 8 10 9 7 5 3 1

Printed and bound in China by Leo Paper Products Ltd

All papers used by Bloomsbury Publishing Plc are natural, recyclable products from wood
grown in well managed forests. The manufacturing processes conform to the environmental
regulations of the country of origin

To find out more about our authors and books visit www.bloomsbury.com
and sign up for our newsletters

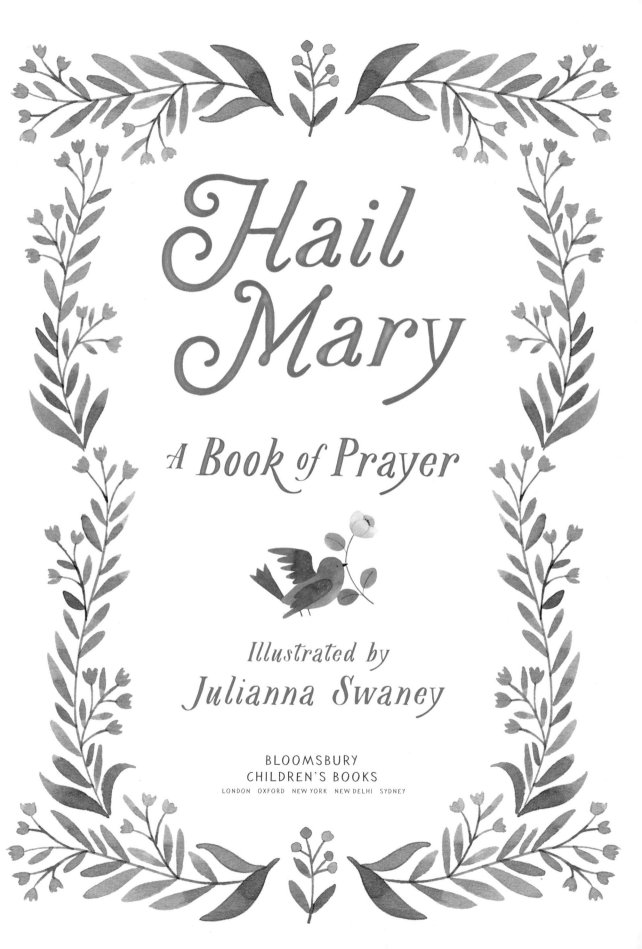

Hail Mary

A Book of Prayer

Illustrated by

Julianna Swaney

BLOOMSBURY
CHILDREN'S BOOKS
LONDON OXFORD NEW YORK NEW DELHI SYDNEY

Introduction

The *Hail Mary* is one of the best-known prayers in the world.

In the prayer, we honour Mary, who is very special because she was chosen by God to be the blessed mother of His son Jesus, our Saviour. We praise Jesus through her and ask her to pray for us to God.

The prayer echoes the words of the Angel Gabriel and St. Elizabeth. 'Hail' means 'Hello' and 'Rejoice and be glad'. When we pray we are saying a happy hello to Mary, and asking her to pray for us now and forever.

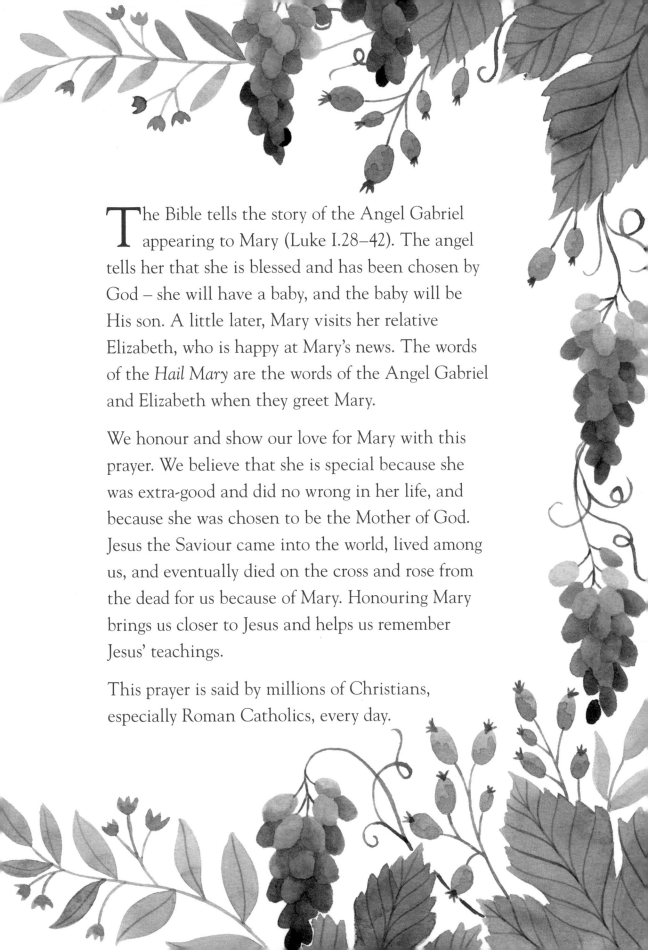

The Bible tells the story of the Angel Gabriel appearing to Mary (Luke I.28–42). The angel tells her that she is blessed and has been chosen by God – she will have a baby, and the baby will be His son. A little later, Mary visits her relative Elizabeth, who is happy at Mary's news. The words of the *Hail Mary* are the words of the Angel Gabriel and Elizabeth when they greet Mary.

We honour and show our love for Mary with this prayer. We believe that she is special because she was extra-good and did no wrong in her life, and because she was chosen to be the Mother of God. Jesus the Saviour came into the world, lived among us, and eventually died on the cross and rose from the dead for us because of Mary. Honouring Mary brings us closer to Jesus and helps us remember Jesus' teachings.

This prayer is said by millions of Christians, especially Roman Catholics, every day.

Hail Mary,
full of
grace,

the Lord is
with thee.

Blessed
art thou
among
women,

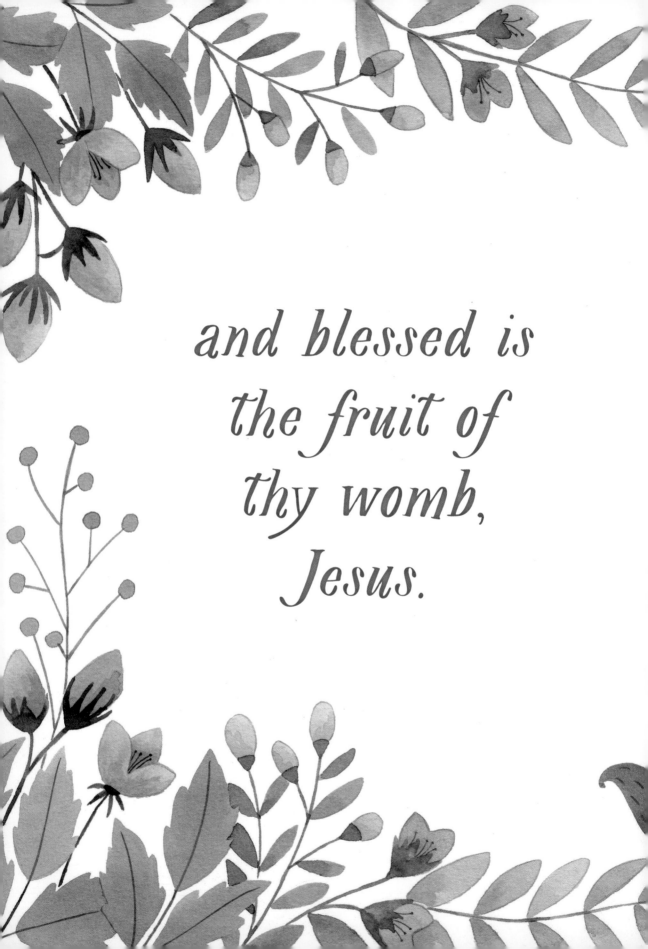

and blessed is
the fruit of
thy womb,
Jesus.

Holy Mary,

Mother
of God,

pray for

us sinners,

now and at the hour
of our death.

Amen.